SOUTHERN LIGHTS
SOUTHERN SHADOWS

poems by

Mary Baker Anderson-Hill

Finishing Line Press
Georgetown, Kentucky

SOUTHERN LIGHTS
SOUTHERN SHADOWS

Copyright © 2016 by Mary Baker Anderson-Hill
ISBN 978-1-944251-60-4   First Edition
All rights reserved under International and Pan-American Copyright Conventions. No part of this book may be reproduced in any manner whatsoever without written permission from the publisher, except in the case of brief quotations embodied in critical articles and reviews.

ACKNOWLEDGMENTS
Published Poems in Southern Lights, Southern Shadows:

"From a Mississippi Porch"   *The Tombigbee Review*
"Southern Lights"   *Atlanta Review*
"Gray Houses"   *Poetry of the Golden Generation*
"The Past Is Ever Present"   *The Lyric,*
"Continuum"   *Poetry of the Golden Generation*

Special Thanks to Kenneth Hamilton York for being Mary Baker Anderson-Hill's Computer Technologist.

Editor: Christen Kincaid

Cover Art: John Andrew Anderson

Author Photo and Interior Photos: Charles William 'Bill' Anderson

Printed in the USA on acid-free paper.
Order online: www.finishinglinepress.com
           also available on amazon.com

Author inquiries and mail orders:
Finishing Line Press
P. O. Box 1626
Georgetown, Kentucky 40324
U. S. A.

Table of Contents

From a Mississippi Porch 1
Southern Lights 2
An Awakening 4
Killing Time 5
Tag-A-Long 6
Epitaph 7
Carrie 8
Great-Great Aunt Susie 10
Mississippi Winter 11
Two Uncle Toms 13
Faces of the Devil 14
The Pond 16
That Mississippi Sound 18
A Homeland Tragedy 19
Gray Houses 21
Seventeen 22
M.S.C.W. 23
Another Emmett Till Story 24
William Raspberry 26
The Forest 28
Let It Rain 29
A Cycle of History 30
Perhaps 32
Continuum 33
A Loving Life 34
Memories 35

*This book is dedicated to
my grandfather, Houston Gilleylen Wood,
who taught me to love poetry as a child
and
to my parents, Hamilton William Baker
and Ellie Elkin Wood Baker,
who taught me to care.*

From a Mississippi Porch

My youth was bound by stories
as voices plied the night and tales were told by starlight
that lulled my world aright. I heard of childhood ventures
and follies of old men, of chases down dark creek beds,
of dogs and quail and kin.

My world was filled with legends
of those both here and gone, which meant they'd gone to glory
for family can't go wrong. Well, one did go to Texas,
but came back all ashamed,
and one to Oklahoma to die in lonely pain.

Several went to the asylum
for being a bit high strung. The rest all just stayed home
content to be unsung. There were tales of how we came here
several hundred years ago, of wagons winding down from Virginia,
of a sailor from a distant shore.

But most of the stories were memories
of other moonlight nights, of hunts and feasts and folly
and how the family set things right.
These tales washed out all evil and made most sinners shine.
They painted life eternal, ridiculous and sublime.

Though I left that storied country,
it still clings to my feet. My heart still beats its waters;
my grave waits in its heat, for I know what earth I came from
and who passed there before, how they lived and died and bore it
from my family's ancient lore.

Southern Lights

Child of the dark my father called me,
born well before rural electrification
found Mississippi's fertile prairie land.
Strange, I don't remember the dark.
I remember lamps with tall glass chimneys,
the medicinal smell of heated coal oil
sucked up braided cloth wicks,
warm light that painted the walls of home.
I remember soot-lined fireplaces,
their andirons heavy with logs and ash
while flames leaped up in reds and gold.

I remember baths in a round tin washtub
pulled cold evenings close to the blazing fire,
the sudden schism as vapor parched,
blistered my front and winter's frozen
tongue licked down my naked spine.
I remember nights under piles of quilts,
a dying bed of coals that flickered to flare up
and light my great-grandmother's portrait
hung in its heavy frame above the mantel.
I remember digging deep beneath the covers
as her eyes seemed to dance in the moving light.

I remember Mama's black iron stove
with its warm fires at the dawn of morning
ready for creations of silken biscuits
that floated out its heavy oven door.
I remember pots of salted hams
that bubbled their heady aroma to the passing wind
and rainbow jars of home grown vegetables

as they steamed in pressure cookers. I remember
baked delights from plums and peaches
that the kitchens of France couldn't touch.
That stove made the lights of Paris seem dull.

On summer days the torrid southern sun
brought more bright heat than ordinary souls
could bear, and even the nights were alight
with a moon that glowed like a muted sun.

Flat on my back in a bed of dew-cooled grass,
as fireflies wavered, sparkled all around,
I could see the globe of evening
curved above my head, its sky alive
with gleaming, glittering stars. In August
hundreds would burn their long-tailed blaze
in vivid streaks across the endless sky.

Nothing could rival that radiant beauty
except the constant beam of my parents'
unfaltering love, always there.
No, Daddy, I was not a child of the dark.

An Awakening

Down our long tree lined driveway
and across the gravel road lived
Jeff Bynum and his children on land
given to his family when slaves

were freed. Our mailboxes stood
side by side. We stopped there on our way
back from town as Jeff walked to our car.
Mr. Hamp, your cows got out in the road,

he said. *I had my boys get them back in.
I thought you'd want to know so you could
walk the fence line. Thank you, Jeff,*
Daddy replied. *I'll do that right away.*

Jeff then leaned towards five year old me.
*Miss Mary Houston, did you have
a good time in town today?* he asked.
Yes Sir, I did, I replied. Then I felt

myself blush and wondered why.
As we moved toward home I thought,
*Nobody white that I know says sir
to a black man, but I've been taught*

to say sir to older men and Jeff is old.
I muttered, *This don't make sense.
Something's wrong with it.
I'll say sir to every old man.*

Killing Time

Iron pot bubbles,
    wire strung down from trees,
board tables readied
    for fall's first chilly breeze.

A red sun hangs witness
    like some bloody mirage
as long knives shine terror
    in tiny swine eyes.

Fat hams tremble;
    hung bodies quake.
Skin will be cut to cracklings
    for tonight's pig-wake.

Wet lips smack in foretaste
    through air rift by death.
Each sharpened blade slices
    taunt tendons, halts breath.

Tag-A-Long

I followed my Daddy when I was a girl.
I helped him herd Jerseys from pastures as I should,
but his birthdays on Christmas put the family in a whirl.

He taught me to milk with my fingers at a furl,
to shoot as many tin cans on posts as I could,
so I copied my Daddy when I was a girl.

Seeking turkeys and nests was more fun than dolls' curls.
We'd gather savory honey from bee trees, in hoods.
I trudged by Daddy like a king's loyal earl.

We listened on radio to the Cardinals hurl
baseballs till winter, then we'd pile up firewood.
One birthday we tramped to hunt quails and squirrels.

I helped my sweet Mother break coconut hulls,
then grate, mix, and taste every bit that would
be his birthday cakes, icings, decorated with swirls.

I treasure life lessons like valuable pearls.
He taught me to share with the misunderstood
as I tagged after Daddy when I was a girl
on his birthdays at Christmas as joyfulness twirled.

Epitaph

Cousin Ben Matthews left Mississippi for Texas long before I was born. He thought to make a fortune, but came back years later in worn overalls, smelled of dirty boxcars, was old, and flat broke. He walked up to his home, now his brother's. He lived out the days of his life in a tall brown rocking chair on his brother's front porch where he spit chewing tobacco, occasionally nodded, but rose at the call for meals. That's where the old usually lived back then, with relatives. The community I grew up in was on a long, country road. The smell of large oak woods, cotton fields, honeysuckle, floated over fences. Scattered farm homes followed along its sides. An ancient cemetery was set among the trees. He finally died and was buried there. After his funeral my Daddy stood at his grave with two farmers he knew. One said, *Well, he was a good old man.* The other rasped, *Yes, he was a good old man, but what in the hell was he good fer?*

Carrie

Carrie was Albert's wife, tall and in charge.
    Albert was a quiet black man who was
ruled by Carrie, my nurse when I was tiny.
    Sometimes she was my babysitter.
When I was five I contacted diphtheria,
    was quarantined for almost a year.
Carrie was found to be the carrier.
    She was quarantined and treated, too.
That gave us something in common.
    Carrie got letters from Eleanor Roosevelt.
I knew this because the mailman spread
    the word all up and down our road.
He was shocked, but nobody else
    seemed to care one way or the other.
One year Carrie decided that she and Albert
    should move to Chicago. I guess
her letters gave her that idea. They moved
    and the next summer Carrie came back
to visit. Carrie walked down and knocked
    on our front door, an unheard of event.
I watched as Mama opened the door.
    She gave Carrie a hug and said she was
so glad to see her. Mama asked her
    to have a seat. Now, my Mama was tall,
beautiful, and considered to be a real lady.
    Nobody ever seemed to think she could do
anything wrong, so I watched carefully.
    Carrie sat down in a rocker on our screened
front porch, which was our summer
    entertainment spot. It was my favorite
place in the world, long and wide,
    with a padded swing at one end,
a wicker couch, several white rocking chairs,
    and four of Mama's flowing green ferns
on white wooden plant tables. Striped rain proof
    pillows and cushions were all around. Often

I propped myself long ways in the swing and read.
    Anyway, Mama excused herself and returned
in a minute with her tea cart, iced tea and all
    that went with it, including her homemade
tea cakes that she seemed to always have on hand.
    I loved that dough! She served and sat
herself down for a nice afternoon visit
    with Carrie. Neither of them seemed to think
that anything was unusual. But I knew it was

Great-Great- Aunt Susie

talked to pictures
when I was a child,
to her mama and her papa,
oil portraits with no smiles.

I thought my aunt was batty
as I listen from my bed
to her early morning visits,
to her haunted promenade.

But now that I've grown older
with my love in his tight cave
I find such conversations
a path beyond the grave.

Mississippi Winter

What's that ole croker sack doing in the ditch?
The wooden school bus skidded as the driver slammed
hard on the brakes. *You all stay right where you are.*
Light was just breaking on a foggy Mississippi morning
that soaked into the bones of those on the bus.
The dirt road was quiet. Stands of cedar trees reared
to their Christmas points along the road's edge, painted
the cold air with their sharp odor. Even the birds
made no dawn sounds. All the children pushed
to one side of the bus to watch as the driver brushed
dried oak leaves off a face that took shape above
a dirt brown coat. *Mr. Hill*, someone whispered.
We all sat down and were as quiet as the birds.
Years later my father finished the story for me.

To us children of the thirties Mr. Hill was a Yankee,
a foreigner from northern Tennessee who came
with his invalid wife to buy depression lost-land.
They hired a fourteen year old needy black girl
from down the road to clean and cook for them daily.
One day Mr. Hill raped her. Afterward she ran home,
her heart full of terror and hate and a secret she couldn't
share for fear her Daddy would get lynched for murder.
All that night she shook hard until the bed springs sang
her song of loss. The next day she claimed to be too sick
inside to go to her job. That morning and the morning after
when everybody had gone to their own piece of work
she waited behind the front door for a knock. She waited
with her Daddy's loaded shotgun held tight in both hands.

When evening came, with sobs the girl told her family
what she had done. Finally the girl's frantic father decided
to trust two white men, men who had always been fair.
He gathered up his warmest coat, ate some fresh cornbread
and peas, kissed his worried wife, walked to Mr. Martin's
and asked him to call Daddy. When together, he told them

what had happened and how his daughter couldn't survive
prison or running away or worse. He asked them to get
him on the midnight train to St. Louis, to put out the word
that he shot Mr. Hill. *I can make it*, he said. *Someday
I can send for my family. Can you keep an eye on them?
See that they have work and no harm comes?* They told him
they would, gave him their few dollars, rolled him like a shot
hound dog in a worn quilt on the car back seat and drove off.

After decades my father was buried in the ancient family cemetery
right off that dirt road. When the family rode away I stayed to be
with Daddy until the dirt was shoveled back in his body's dark trench.
When I left I passed the gray, dog-trot house where the girl's family
had once lived. An old woman was rocking on the front porch.
On an impulse I pulled over and walked to the porch. I asked
if she knew the girl. *I'm her auntie*, was the soft reply. I asked
if she knew the story about the killing and my Daddy's part
in helping out. *Girl,* she said, *we black people have always
known that story. Just the whites was ignorant. Mr. Hamp was
a good man just like her Daddy was. Did you ever hear
from Belle after they left?* I asked. *Well,* she replied,
*one time some years back her sister came down. She wasn't
with her. Hate and mistrust still running stormy in her heart,
but a little feeling for home still. She asked her sister to bring
her back a rock from the yard. A broken one like her.*

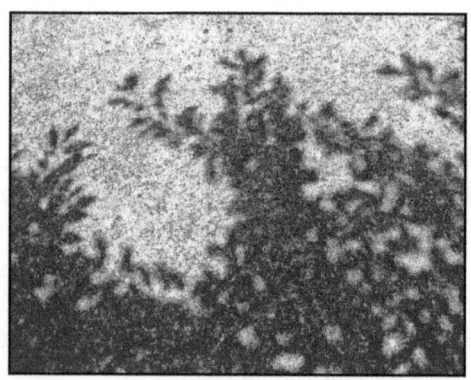

Two Uncle Toms

One was white. One was black and a childhood
    slave of my great grandfather. One was
the father of my three cousins with whom I played
    daily. Uncle Tom Smith and Aunt Harriet
had a well with a wooden bucket and a rope
    to pull up their water. They had a half open
grave in their woods. We liked to play there and
    hear the stories Uncle Tom would tell about
long ago. One summer their children came home
    from St. Louis to visit and built a new, large
room on their parent's shotgun cabin. Uncle Tom
    and Aunt Harriet never moved in. When
fall came they put their cotton there until they
    could take it to the gin, but in the meantime
they let us jump in it. Uncle Tom Smith said their barn
    was too rickety to hold cotton anymore, so we
decided to make use of it. We freed a claw hammer
    and a can of nails from my Uncle Tom
Wood's barn, pried off old boards from the back of

Uncle Tom Smith's barn, carried them across the road to
    Uncle Tom Wood's 'little woods'
which separated his home from all of our fields.
    We proceeded to build a long longed for tree house.
About half way through we saw Uncle Tom Smith in a trot,
    white hair, bent shoulders, walking cane, and all,
toward Uncle Tom Wood's house. Soon they walked
    purposefully toward us. We thought oh, oh,
for Uncle Tom Wood stopped and striped a long switch off
    a handy bush. Very soon we had torn down our
almost finished tree house, paraded back across the road
    in single file with boards over each child's shoulder
and carefully nailed every old board back on Uncle Tom
    Smith's barn while both uncles watched.
Uncle Tom Smith repeatedly said he just couldn't
    believe them chillun would do that.
        By then, neither could we.

Faces of the Devil

Our pastor was in trouble. He and his wife had insisted that their black cook eat at the family table, something that wasn't done in the forties down South. An elderly ruling elder, as he called himself, from a small, very rural church had walked into the manse without knocking, as was his custom, saw this and roared. The frightened cook jumped and ran home terrified for her life. The elder shook his finger in the pastor's face and stormed out to spread the word of our minister's behavior. That night the Ku Klux Klan burned a flaming cross in the pastor's front yard. This frightened his three small children who thought ghosts had come to burn their home down and to drag all of their bodies off to the grave yard. As they sobbed their parents held them close and explained that the strange men wouldn't hurt them. The minister silently prayed that this was true, both for his family and for their cook.

Mississippi heat boiled down as Mama and I sat in the car and tensely listened. The elders of our Mississippi Presbytery, all men then, orated in the main building here on our youth campground high on a wooded hill with the ancient Tombigbee River almost circling it far below. This peaceful spot, one that often echoed with the laughter of children, was disturbed by loud voices pushing out open windows. The dogwoods' white, cross-shaped blossoms hung their heads, but their scent filled the air, erasing harshness as best it could. I picked several yellow honeysuckle blooms so Mama and I could suck out the summer sweetness. Finally, we heard a motion to dismiss Rev. Sylvester and we cringed. Then we heard Daddy's soft voice. He asked that before the vote everyone bow their heads and in a few minutes of silence think about what Jesus would do. In a short time the vote was called. Rev. Sylvester stayed.

This cowardly Klan, dangerous as they hid their faces under sheets, invaded our winding country road, our peaceful black and white community only once. Early one morning the phone rang to tell us that an African American church near my Grandmother Baker's home where Daddy grew up had been burned to the ground that night by the Klan. After Daddy finished milking, a twice a day necessity, he climbed into his pickup truck and started down the road. He stopped at each family's home, black or white, to ask for a donation of money or labor to rebuild. At a few houses he stated that he never wanted to hear of anything like this happening in our community again. The small wooden church was rebuilt by the people of the community by the next Sunday service.

The Pond

This water, dappled liquid glass,
rich with muck where tall grass grows
holds life within, without its folds.
Fresh green from trees drifts slowly down
without a sound, without a sound.
The sun must search between each leaf
to find this spot, this silvered pond.
Serene, it holds life in its coil,
in summer's broth, in living brew,
and on its surface swims a goose.

Gray body moves on silent oars
by blossoms drifting slowly on,
by dragonfly and flitting moth.
He cuts a V in burnished gold
and fills the heavy, shadowed air
with long, low calls for his lost mate,
his mate who searched within the mud
when turtles stole her nesting eggs.
She cried as though her heart would break,
Then sank into the sucking mire.

But still her lover gives his call
in hopes she might rise up again,
though lady goose and shattered eggs
have swirled to marsh, and mud, and mire,
for life this water takes and breeds.
It sucks away deep in its depth.
It slowly works in silt and gloom.
The dark, the glistening, silent pond
grasps life within, without its folds.
It holds the gander's nesting bird.

Then from the great heart in the marsh
there grew some grass which sprouted green,
when ripened fell upon the pond

and lay all golden on its sheen
until some geese as they flew by
fed to their fill. One laid an egg.
Enriched by grain from dead heart's blood
it hatched a gosling fair and wild
who gave some low and lonesome cries
    until her gander glided by.

That Mississippi Sound

Warm earth that broods
long, too long. Its words
move like sweet molasses
in a slow cadence of time,
of connected blood.
Sounds that came from Africans
in chains, from the British Isles
when the Hanovers reigned.
Words that seep quietly
from voices Mississippi bred,
words as thick as its mud.

Homeland Tragedy
World War II

Off the school bus
All alone
A telegram
taped to our door
I stared
The Army Air Force regrets
First Lieutenant Andrew Wood
My young Uncle Andrew!

At the bottom handwritten
'Gone to be with Mama'
Sharp sobs
piled their pointed
edges against my ribs
into my stomach's
blackest pit
Tears exploded
Mucus poured
from my nose
Finally
I gathered my feet
beneath me
Heavy arms dragged
as I stumbled off
seeking comfort

My uncle's wife
smiled, patted
Her form
filled the room
Words seeped
into my fog—
>*don't*
>*his*
>*accident*
>*death.*

Silently I wailed
My head pounded

I crept back to my empty house
coiled tightly in my bed
Horrible visions slithered
through my brain—
Gory pieces grated
inside my swollen eyelids—
sliced inside my heart

Gray Houses

Gray and worn old houses,
shells of times gone by,
settle ever closer
as earth shifts them more awry.

They're filled with forlorn groans
and whispers that defy
the last of those who left them
with a glad goodbye.

The ones who left the houses
now walk crowded city streets
learned, and lean, and harried,
and burning to retreat

to the old, gray houses
that stand in the fields,
ones they can't push under
for fear they'll lose what's real

for with those ancient houses
memories will die
like a summer's wild blackberries
dried beneath the sky.

Seventeen

A shaft of light broke through
the open kitchen door
and beckoned out,
out into the world.
Unfurl.
Hope was born with fear
that somewhere there was strength
to walk beyond
to where the light
was coming from.

M.S.C.W.
'49-'53

Oh, hail to thee—we rally to thee,
to the yellow and white—all girls
old maid's gate—walking backwards
big sisters—professors—house mothers
wonderful friends—devouring knowledge
triple dating—or chaperone—no cars
campus benches that dates couldn't sit on
in dorms by ten—lights out by eleven
Mississippi State boys—panty raids
speech—now able to hold an audience
Theatre Guild—stage manager—fun
campus wide Zouave Drill—beautiful
Westminster Fellowship—Outreach
trombone in the college orchestra
art—dinner invitation to Faculty Club
discussed ending segregation in Mississippi
science like never before—loved history
summer jobs in the rural reaches of Presbytery
in a settlement house in Chicago
Future Teachers of America president
practice teaching—excited about job
hard to leave friends, plays, concerts,
experiences each day held here
left the girl behind—became an adult
wondering about life with men around
the final march—the Chain of Magnolias

Another Emmett Till Story

How lucky can I be? I am a teacher in my first job.
I love these wonderful kids!
Greenwood, the Mississippi Delta, music, fun,
I wonder why I get paid to do something I enjoy so much!
But something awful just happened. A child killed.
A black child named Emmett Till.

He was only fourteen. Murdered, mutilated in Money, Mississippi.
I teach pupils from there.
Now words are being whispered about who killed him.
They say he whistled at the storekeeper's wife.
Didn't he know better? *No, he was from Chicago,*
his grandmother's visitor. Somebody dared him.

All the youngsters ran away when he did it.
Nobody thought he would.
Why would somebody get so upset about that?
Maybe we don't know all of it.
Today's paper says a jury will be called
right away to try those men who killed him.

Good, maybe we'll have some peace now.
Surely, they will go to jail. *I wouldn't be so sure.*
The father of one of my pupils is on the jury.
He's a really good guy.
He had me out to his plantation for dinner once.
He'll see to it that there's justice.

I wouldn't be too sure about that if I were you.
I can't believe it! That jury let them go.
Everybody knew they did it.
Maybe everybody thought that child needed to be killed.
No! Everybody here isn't like that. I'll talk to my class,
tell them God made us all. We have to care about one another.

You may get fired.
I don't want to stay.
Not anymore.

William Raspberry

grew up
by our home town
a tiny place
in rural Mississippi
we must have
passed on the street
hundreds of times
but we didn't trade
in the same stores
or sing
in the same choir
or drink
at the same fountain
or study
at the same school
or march
in the same band
or sit together
at the movies
or swim together
at the park
or play ball together
with friends
or eat together
anywhere
our mamas and daddies
didn't know each other
it was like
we had blinders on
or lived
in two dimensions
on some science fiction show
we grew up
in the mid-nineteen hundreds
he was black
I was white

I read later
in one of his
nationally syndicated columns
that he lived there
and thought
what a loss
I never knew him
and I grew up
by William Raspberry's
tiny home town

The Forest

If I could paint a picture for all the world to see
I'd show these fallen blossoms beneath this stately tree.

I'd like to share this forest with each who is deprived,
that all might know the beauty of a land so uncontrived.

The ground is rich and heavy with decay from ages past;
here giants entwine together to reach sun's fiery blast.

Some blues and greens are golden, intense from Orpheus' glow,
while in hushed, soft shaded crannies lichen and violets grow.

The air somehow is sweeter, its music a running brook
that cuts through hills and hollows or hides in a tangled nook.

I know the trees saw natives and woodsmen with their guns;
later the edges saw farmers baring black earth to the sun.

But now comes a sound of destruction as civilization closes in,
saws with a taste for timber as rampant as original sin.

Someone paint this picture quickly so all the world can know
these woods, here filled with wonder, before their final throe.

Let It Rain

The pond is half-dry. A wide
berm of wrinkled earth
surrounds it. Where water bugs
once played by the hundreds
an occasional frog's head
pops up in hopes of food,
a bite of bug I imagine.
Even the birds are gone.
Reeds and weeds will sprout
to form an inner bank. This
has happened so often lately
that the ground seems to parch
as soon as the sun sees
its muddy face. No sign of turtles.
Could they have crawled
to the creek below? Well,
I will do a dance,
chant and find a drum
to beat and if the frogs
would croak in great
k-rumps that might help.
If not, croak may
take on new meaning.

A Cycle of History

by a large magnolia tree
with bowl-like blossoms
heavy with perfume
stood a southern saltbox
old when I was born
it stretched its lofty ceilings
far from a northern sea
with its loaded ships
and twisted records
its walls wore history
a few half-filled bullet holes
propelled there
by Grant's raiders
as they plundered their way
through Mississippi

in the woods behind
a sunken trail
here and there
the old Grant road
where blood was shed
deeper into the trees
where a mockingbird sang
a hidden burial ground
small, surrounded
by an iron fence
inside three graves
and an ancient cedar tree
wounded by a bowie knife
plunged deep into its heart
in the faded past
slowly the tree devours it
here a matriarch
great great great great
grandmother Jane Baker
mother of the young men

who followed worn trails
through black forests
for week after week
like hungry bears
seeking their own territory
in a land still filled
with heartbroken Chickasaw cries
here the men settled
here they began their own tribe
nearly two hundred years ago

now the home is gone
but for ages this new tribe
gathered here annually
the first Sunday in August
that short time
when crops are laid by
as generations passed
these reunions
with their tables of food
with their laughter
camaraderie and joy
marked us all as one

these well-off brothers
with their white skin
moved into
Chickasaw land
with black slaves
grew fields rich with cotton
fertilized by red anger
and black blood
never repaid

Perhaps

minds can build a reasoned path
when open hearts expand
to mix all reaching thoughts with love
then heaven can grow in man

Continuum

Each path of life is filled with twists and turns.
From mayflies flights to primates' balanced stance
We wind through thorns and pause by flowing ferns.

Perhaps once paths were straight, as mankind yearns,
But prior the time a hand first flung a lance
Each path of life was filled with twists and turns.

It seems both pain and joy of beauty churn
A gladsome, madding mix as paths advance
To wind through thorns and pause by flowing fern

While deep within us all a longing burns
To know if God guides fate or if by chance
Each path of life is filled with twists and turns.

I'd guess whatever lesson creatures learn
This truth will stand: mortals, in dissonance,
Will wind through thorns and pause by flowing fern

Till ending. As the eras leave their ruin
And earth winds down to fling her final dance
All paths of life will weave with twists and turn
To fall through thorns then rest by flowing ferns.

A Loving Life

When youth I lived a loving life
of joy, of angst, of growth.
Though bound with care
I stretched my skin
until the boundaries broke.

I dwelled, a fledgling, in myself
exploring earth about.
The right to be the I in me
was powerful company.

For rearing years my life was rich,
with centers I adored;
as peaks and lows would find my door,
day's needs would form my floor.

When age approached
we linked our hands,
their union mortal balm,
but now I lead a mirrored life,
grown darker since you've gone.

Memories

The past is ever present,
whether invited or scorned.
It slips inside a moment,
joyfully or scarcely borne.

It lives forever coiled,
any instant lures a strike.
As age unwinds life's timepiece,
nostalgia, assassin like,

slays the precious minutes
that augment a fleeting life.
Memories erupt like mice
as the piper plays his fife.

Mary Houston Baker Anderson-Hill was born on her family's farm in northeast Mississippi during the depression and the time of segregation. She graduated from Mississippi State College for Women and began teaching in Greenwood, Mississippi. After teaching in Nokomis, Florida, she received her Masters Degree from Teachers College, Columbia University, New York, NY.

During this time she married John Crowell Anderson from Montclair, New Jersey, followed him to Tuscaloosa, Alabama and around the eastern United States as General Electric moved them with their children from place to place. When they settled in Cobb County, Georgia, she returned to teaching while looking after the children, Bill, Mary, and John, and her husband. She adored all.

She attended the University of Georgia for her Specialist Degree and became a school administrator. After losing her beloved husband to cancer she married an old friend and mentor, her old age companion, the late Dr. Henry Hill. She is the proud grandmother of three, Kenneth, Sophia, and Emily, and spends her autumn years writing poetry and working on a book, *Silent Voices, How to Improve Poverty Schools*.

www.ingramcontent.com/pod-product-compliance
Lightning Source LLC
Chambersburg PA
CBHW051704040426
42446CB00009B/1302